"Through scripture, metaphors and the Christian giants of history, Nagy shows us in *Trust: A Perspective on God's Will* that discerning God's will for our lives is more than knowing what's around the corner. God's will is for us to trust him through the thick and thin, the good and the bad, but particularly the trials of life. This is what leads to holiness. We are to be patient and know God is working in our lives for His good and our good. My favorite phrases to hold onto as I learn to trust God with my life are: "an experienced gardener will never damage a fruit tree by pruning it,' and 'the goldsmith has to place the gold in the hottest part of the fire.'"

Rachel Britton
Speaker, Author and Blogger

"It is hard not to be moved by Timothy Nagy's passion for his topic and his own trust in God's desire for our sanctification, helpfully defined as the process in which we become more like Jesus Christ. Mr. Nagy's brief but deep dive into biblical theology will reward those who are new to the faith as well as the more seasoned disciple in need of spiritual refreshment from a young and welcome voice."

The Rt. Rev. A. Robert Hirschfeld
Bishop of the Episcopal Diocese of
New Hampshire

"Timothy Nagy provokes spiritual introspection to galvanize our trust in the character of God. His book delivers an honest, straightforward approach for all Believers who seek fulfillment in their spiritual journey."

Archbishop Timothy Paul, S.T.D.
International Communion Of
The Holy Christian Orthodox Church

"*Trust: A Perspective on God's Will* provides a roadmap to the frequently-asked and intensely-felt question, 'What is God's will?' Drawing from a wide range of voices in the Christian tradition and ever dependent on Scripture, Nagy does not suggest a short jaunt to an easy answer, but a lifelong journey to the right answer: God's will is to trust unto holiness. I will be glad to put this into the hands of my students and parishioners who are in the midst of asking this question."

Amy Peeler
Associate Professor of New Testament,
Wheaton College and
Associate Rector, St. Mark's Episcopal Church,
Geneva, IL

TRUST
A Perspective
on God's Will

TIMOTHY NAGY

© 2018

Published in the United States by Nurturing Faith Inc.,
Macon GA, www.nurturingfaith.net.

Library of Congress Cataloging-in-Publication Data is available.

ISBN 978-1-63528-050-0

Cover and interior art by zoom-zoom.

TABLE OF CONTENTS

Preface...ix

Introduction...1

Discerning God's Will 7

Holiness 13

Discipline...23

Obedience 41

Promises..49

Patience...57

Trust as God's Will 65

Conclusion...73

Notes 81

I have sat down to write a preface for this book a few times now, and I have found it challenging to convey what I want without being too polarizing. I also want to carefully set a tone that is conversational, easygoing, and ecumenical. So to you, my reader, before you dive into this book, I hope that you will consider the following train of thought.

Belief and trust are key differentiating factors in Christianity. Belief is judging something to be factual. Believing the gospel of Jesus Christ is the first critical step in Christian life. However, just as James writes that faith without works is dead, I would say that belief without trust is dead. Belief indicates that one is convinced of God's existence, but what's next? What can one do with such an amazing reality? You guessed it—one can trust. Trust is a means for activating belief. Trust is putting faith into action. Trust is the difference between knowing

Jesus is there and following him. Furthermore, trust is not an aloof and dogmatic theological concept tucked away somewhere in the church archives. Rather, trust is accessible to all and is essential to everyday Christian life.

Trusting God, though essential, is difficult—sometimes extremely difficult. The shadow of death, the rapids of divorce, the dagger of heartache, the chasm of addiction, the stupor of confusion, the precipice of disability, the darkness of depression, the deluge of anxiety, the torrent of disease—life is marked by suffering. As the disciples said, "We must go through many hardships to enter the kingdom of God" (Acts 14:22, NIV). But how can one get through these storms? Once again, you guessed it—one can trust. And trusting is not only for enduring trials. One can trust God at all times (see, e.g., Ps 62:8). In fact, as the title indicates, I am going to try to convince you that trusting in God is God's will.

I will leave you with one more thought before you move on. Much of what I am getting at with this book is a perspective, or an attitude perhaps, for approaching life. For a Christian, going along with the crowd will never cut it. Other philosophies will not work. Following Jesus is still radical, still difficult, yet still life-giving and the most practical decision one can make. Søren Kierkegaard, the great nineteenth-century Danish philosopher, puts the matter this way: "'For,' says common sense, 'a fanatic is a fanatic. Bad enough. But seriously to…become his disciple is the greatest possible madness. There is only one possible way of being madder than a madman: it is the higher madness of attaching oneself in all seriousness to a madman, regarding him as a wise man.'"[1] I have been engaging with this higher madness for some time now, and it has caused a paradigm shift in my very being. The mind is where that shift starts, and I do not think it ever ends. Therefore, let us search this great madness and see if we might find some wisdom after all.

Timothy Nagy, Riverdale, NY
December 1, 2017

INTRODUCTION

This little book is a product of my attempt to discern God's will. During my discernment I have experienced everything from deep confusion to freeing contentment. The pages that follow are not a direct reflection on these experiences—I plan to present those in another volume. Instead, I have compiled the most essential Bible passages, prayers, and writings that have helped me gain a new understanding. These words have gradually shifted my understanding of God's will for his people, have sustained me throughout times of despair, and have put me on the narrow path going ahead (see Matt 7:13). They have taught me the importance of discipline, obedience, and patience. They have shown me a new approach toward suffering, the power of prayer, and the expectation of tension. These words have convinced me to be excited for the future as I look forward to God's promises.

By chance the extra-biblical material I have included is of a confidently ecumenical flavor. Anglican, Baptist, Calvinist, Catholic, Greek Orthodox, Lutheran, and Reformed thought are all incorporated. Each has helped me to grapple with different topics and to approach them biblically. I believe Christianity goes far beyond any and all earthly polity and side with this thought from Gordon Smith: "Evangelicals are increasingly insistent that conversion is not ultimately to the church but to Christ and his kingdom, and that therefore the kingdom and not the church is the focus of mission. The church is only a means to the end."[2] Being a member of a strong community of faith is essential to living an authentic Christian life. God calls us to be one unified body, and that is reflected in each church, each community of believers striving together to keep in step with the Spirit. Church leaders are appointed to shepherd God's flock. These leaders are constantly engaging in the gospel-centric mission of creating, building, and strengthening trust in God through Jesus Christ. Given this dynamic, Smith's note that the "church is only a means to the end" is of great value. In other words, the practices and understandings may vary amongst the denominations, but the goal is the same: hallowed be thy name.

My thinking on the topic of trust began when I realized I have free will—when I truly comprehended the vast amount of choices I can make. This idea challenged me, and I desperately wanted to make the correct and optimal choice in every situation. All I wanted was for God to replace my will with his will. That desire has not changed, but my understanding of how that might happen has. This little book presents my perspective, based on biblical and theological reflection, on God's will and his gift to us that allows us to pursue it—namely, trust.

The Greek word for faith, trust, and reliability is Πίστις or *pistis*. Many translate *pistis* as "faith," but I offer that translating *pistis* as "trust" allows for a much better understanding because it conveys relationship with God. Faith has gradually come to mean belief that God exists. This is a product of the popularization and acceptance of atheism, the increasingly interfaith landscape, and the promotion of a clash between science and religion. Belief is an absolutely paramount aspect of Christian life since belief initiates one's relationship with God. However, a relationship with God must surpass belief. Faith is a noun. One can *have* faith, but one cannot *faith* God. Trust is a verb; it makes faith an action. One can trust God. Therefore, trust gives us a better framework for thinking about *pistis* because it conveys action and relationship. To trust is to act upon that original belief in God, establishing a link that can either grow stronger or fade away over time. A great way of thinking about this link is to consider the metaphor Jesus presents in John 15:1–8 of the vine and the branches. This metaphor holds trust at the pinnacle of Christian life as trust enables one to do God's will—that is what I aim to show throughout this book.

I recommend keeping a Bible close by as you read. The endnotes at the end of the book include additional verses on the topic at hand that you may want to investigate. For longer passages I have included a snippet of the text, but it will be most helpful to read the entire passage from your Bible.

DISCERNING GOD'S WILL

Romans 12:1–2

I appeal to you therefore, brothers, by the mercies of God, to present your bodies as a living sacrifice, holy and acceptable to God, which is your spiritual worship. Do not be conformed to this world, but be transformed by the renewal of your mind, that by testing you may discern what is the will of God, what is good and acceptable and perfect. (Rom 12:1–2)

Classically understood, Christian life begins with justification—e.g., being saved, conversion, regeneration, rebirth, surrender, born again, born from above, repent and believe, baptism, metanoia, Spirit baptism—and after that it is a process called sanctification—e.g., discipleship, refiner's fire, perfection, the narrow way, epistrophe, the highway of holiness. To be justified means to be declared righteous by God because one has entered into a relationship with Jesus by believing and trusting in Jesus. Therefore, God has judged that person to be holy because God sees Jesus in those who believe and trust Jesus. To be sanctified means to gradually reflect Jesus' holiness in one's own life through God's Spirit and God's Word. In other words, God works in those he has already declared to be holy to actually display holiness in their behavior.[3] One way of looking at it is to think about citizenship. Justification is like becoming a citizen of a country. It is a new status. Sanctification is similar to learning and obeying the laws, learning and participating in the culture, and learning and speaking the language of that country. One cannot be more or less of a citizen, but one can display their citizenship gradually over time through committing to one's new country. Similarly, holiness is a legal status with God. One cannot be more holy, but one can display one's holiness gradually over time by trusting in God and committing to his ways instead of one's old ways. The perspective laid out in this book is particularly directed at those who have been justified and are now in the process of being sanctified.[4] It is a perspective for Christians who are seeking God's will for their life—their calling, their vocation, their purpose.

Paul's charge to the Romans in the above passage is one of the best places to start the discernment process. First, he mentions the role of the body in this pursuit. One must offer one's body as a sacrifice as proper spiritual worship of God. This means putting others first, putting God's commandments first, hating and fighting against sin, and living a moral lifestyle. One must embrace Paul's words from the very next chapter to the Romans, the same words Augustine embraced at his conversion (see Rom 13:13–14). This task is achievable through trust and obedience, which will be discussed later.

For now I will turn to verse 2. Here, Paul outlines the entire process of sanctification—the process of becoming holy—which is God's ultimate will for his people. This process is a gradual reorientation to God in all aspects of life, and it starts with the mind. One must no longer be conformed to this world! The mind becomes a prisoner to patterns of thought that can be "good," "bad," or "neutral," but Christians are called to go beyond any sort of earthly reason and trust in God's Word, "believing it to be a stronger foundation than all the securities in the world."[5] Christians must be serious about Jesus' teachings and live by them. Each mind on this earth is constantly bombarded with pleas for prioritization. Weight loss, makeup, clothing, college, getting married—people obsess over these topics and set them as their top priority. However, Christians desperately need to prioritize following Jesus. I love how Søren Kierkegaard speaks of the disciples following a madman.[6] Sometimes it may seem counterintuitive to trust Jesus' teachings, but it will always be the best choice.

My conclusion, which is primarily Scripture-driven, is that God sanctifies his people through discipline and that the role of each person in this process will always be to trust God. This will become clear in the following sections. Another way of putting it is this threefold sequence of questions: (1) What is God's will? (2) How does God achieve his will? (3) How can I respond? The answers, which I will explain, are: (1) For his people to be holy; (2) through discipline; and (3) trust God through obedience, patience, and knowing God's promises. These three points will guide the rest of this exploration. Everything culminates with point three, the human role within the sanctification process—trust. Trust is faith in action—it is essentially the verb "to faith." To endure God's sanctifying discipline one will need obedience, patience, and God's promises.

1 Thessalonians 4:1–8

Finally, then, brothers, we ask and urge you in the Lord Jesus, that as you received from us how you ought to walk and to please God, just as you are doing, that you do so more and more. For you know what instructions we gave you through the Lord Jesus. For this is the will of God, your sanctification…. For God has not called us for impurity, but in holiness. Therefore whoever disregards this, disregards not man but God, who gives his Holy Spirit to you. (1 Thess 4:1–3, 7–8)

God's will for all is clearly sanctification.[7] So why am I putting all of this emphasis on trust?

It is because people cannot sanctify themselves. God is the sanctifier—the purifier, the refiner, the perfecter—but his people have a different role. Sanctification is God's persistent work in his people, and their best response is trusting in that work. I think it makes sense to think about it this way, too: God does God's will—God's people trust that he is doing it.

I used to be under the impression that God would reveal his will to me and that it would be some specific lifelong task that I would then be able to work toward. Now I understand that God's will is for his people to surrender their lives and to trust in him completely, and in Jesus Christ, so that he might make them his holy people. This makes clarity a dangerous thing to request. God has designed his relationship with his people on the foundation of trust so he can be in control and gradually build on the holy and righteous status that they have through their relationship with Jesus. If he were to provide great detail about what we are to do with our lives and where we will be in twenty years, it may be incredibly daunting to have a specific task to execute. What if God told you to leave your family and plant a church in a war-torn country? One could hope that one would be able to do so, but it would be very difficult. Does the story of Jonah come to mind?[8] God may have something like this planned for us in five years, and he will prepare us over those years so we are ready to accept, to the point where he will be the one acting.

There is a story I have heard about a conversation between Mother Teresa and a philosopher named John Kavanaugh. Kavanaugh was at a crossroads in his life, wondering what he should do. When she asked him what he wanted, he said, "Clarity, pray that I have clarity." And she replied, "No. I will not do that. Clarity is the last thing you are clinging to and must let go of." He was confused because it seemed to him that she had clarity. But she laughed in reply: "I have never had clarity; what I have always had is trust. So I will pray that you will trust God."[9] The only clarity one can lean on is God's Word—the truth.

Practical Holiness

a) Holiness is the habit of being of one mind with God, according as we find His mind described in Scripture. It is the habit of agreeing in God's judgement—hating what He hates—loving what He loves—and measuring everything in this world by the standard of His Word. He who most entirely agrees with God, he is the most holy man.

b) A holy man will endeavour to shun every known sin, and to keep every known commandment. He will have a decided bent of mind toward God, a hearty desire to do His will—a greater fear of displeasing Him than of displeasing the world, and a love to all His ways. He will feel what Paul felt when he said, "I delight in the law of

God after the inward man" (Rom. 7:22), and what David felt when he said, "I esteem all Thy precepts concerning all things to be right, and I hate every false way" (Psalm 119:128).[10]

J. C. Ryle was the first Anglican bishop of Liverpool in the nineteenth century. The two characteristics of holiness above are the first two on a list of twelve Ryle included in a famous sermon on holiness. I wanted to include these points because the first point provides a clear link back to the renewal of the mind, and the second point has important practical considerations.

"Holiness is the habit of being of one mind with God"—I very much appreciate how Ryle phrases this statement. His use of the word "habit" is critically important because it illustrates that sanctification is gradual. Habits come about through repetition—everything from nail-biting to exercising. The repetition of trusting in God, of turning to him in all circumstances—whether to praise or weep or pray—is what forms this habit of holiness. People can choose to form this habit or to turn toward something else. It is a matter of trusting that God's commandments really should be followed instead of what one's own mind thinks is right. This is a helpful way of thinking about the sanctification process as a whole. It also relates to Kierkegaard's sense of "higher madness." Sometimes commandments might seem mad, but one must agree with God that they are right. One must renew one's mind and replace one's preconceived notions with God's laws—God's expert strategies for displaying holiness.

Ryle's second point is also essential because it denotes the further connection between the mind and the body. When one is dedicated to the human role in the process of sanctification, one will see one's trust overflow from intellect to action. The most direct way is in regard to sin. One will begin to hate sin as God hates sin, and one will begin to fight it. One will seek out and keep all of God's commandments, knowing they sustain life and act as lampposts on the narrow path. One will realize just how marvelous a blessing his commandments are, delighting in them as Paul did and finding all of them right as David did. Ultimately, one will understand why the sheep-shepherd metaphor is used so often in Scripture and why one needs God's commandments to replace wandering with direction.

Holiness traditionally means "set apart" or "sheer difference from everything else." These are helpful ways of thinking about the goal of the sanctification process. God's will for his people is for them to be set apart for whatever purpose God has for them. To be made holy is to be made in the image of Jesus Christ. Christian life is the journey to that goal. Christians display holiness in their behavior by trusting, obeying, waiting, and totally relying on God. This attitude toward God is one God cultivates in his people. It shows that out of the countless options to choose from, one has chosen God's way. Given my love of sports, I often think about this within the dynamic of a coach-player relationship. If the player wants playing time, the player must buy into the coach's system. This means being a good teammate, preparing for games by practicing and watching film, fitting into the culture of the locker room, and being willing to play wherever the coach thinks is best. Usually if the player has this attitude toward the coach and the team, the coach will take notice and put the player in the best places to succeed. I think it is quite similar in Christian life. It is not about knowing our specific position at the beginning of the season; it is putting in the time to know God's "system"—his commandments, promises, and mission—and trusting that God will put those dedicated to him in places to glorify him and contribute to building up his kingdom.

I think of holiness in two ways: essence and disposition. Essence pertains to ontology or being while disposition refers to attitude or action. This differentiation has helped me think about how holiness flows from God to his people. It begins with God's holy essence. God is holy as a being. He is set apart from everything else. From God's essence comes his holy disposition, which is complete dedication to his people—essentially faithfulness and love.[11] From God's disposition comes the gift of Jesus. Once God's people enter into a relationship with Jesus, they are declared holy, and God works in them through this relationship to reflect that status in their behavior. In this declaration, God makes his people his sons and daughters, and he is their father. As their father, God raises them to reflect that defining characteristic of holiness just as Jesus does. This is the attitude of the player described in the player-coach relationship. In responding to God's love, one must also have a disposition of dedication to God, displayed through the renewal of the mind by trust, obedience, patience, hope, love, and all of the other biblical virtues.

God's holy essence gives way to his holy disposition, and for his people it is the same because of their relationship with Jesus and their status of holiness. People are not inherently holy, but they become holy when they are united to Jesus. Then through the renewal of their minds, they begin to cultivate a holy disposition of virtuous commitment to God. Trust is what establishes and grows one's relationship with God. As Ryle notes, "Holiness comes from Christ. It is the result of vital union with Him. It is the fruit of being a living branch of the true Vine."[12] Once again, John 15:1–8 presents a great illustration for this dynamic. One can only be a branch on the vine if one is already holy, and one's fruitfulness is contingent upon one's relationship to the vine, Jesus. The gardener, God, prunes the branch to maximize its fruitfulness. This pruning is discipline, the next subject in this exploration.

DISCIPLINE

Hebrews 12:1–14

Therefore…let us also lay aside every weight, and sin which clings so closely, and let us run with endurance the race that is set before us, looking to Jesus, the founder and perfecter of our faith [*pistis*], who for the joy that was set before him endured the cross…. Have you forgotten the exhortation that addresses you as sons?

"My son, do not regard lightly the discipline of the Lord,

nor be weary when reproved by him.

For the Lord disciplines the one he loves,

and chastises every son whom he receives."

It is for discipline that you have to endure. God is treating you as sons. For what son is there whom his father does not discipline? If you are left without discipline, in which all have participated, then you are illegitimate children and not sons. Besides this, we have had earthly fathers who disciplined us and we respected them…. They disciplined us for a short time as it seemed best to them, but he disciplines us for our good, that we may share his holiness. For the moment all discipline seems painful rather than pleasant, but later it yields the peaceful fruit of righteousness to those who have been trained by it…. Strive for peace with everyone, and for the holiness without which no one will see the Lord. (Heb 12:1–2, 5–9a, 10–11, 14)

To do his sanctifying work, God employs discipline, also known as reproof, rebuke, instruction, training, and chastisement. This is where the rubber meets the road, and if one is without trust, everything will fall apart. Paul wrote these words to the Hebrews to indicate to them that their sufferings were not because of disfavor with God, but because God was loving them as their father. James writes: "Count it all joy, my brothers, when you meet trials of various kinds, for you know that the testing of your faith produces steadfastness. And let steadfastness have its full effect, that you may be perfect and complete, lacking in nothing" (1:2–4). Having this perspective regarding trials is made possible by God's promises, which will be explored in a later section.

Through my reflections it has become clear to me that tension is part of the very foundation of life, excellence, and progress. In a piece of music, resolve is not possible without dissonance. The "finer things in life," such as fine wines, spirits, and cheeses, are only that way through aging. Athletes become stronger through training, tearing muscles and building them back up. Gold and silver are refined in fire. Fine articles of clothing are held together by the tensions in the fabric. Wood and stone have to be cut and sanded to become homes and buildings. The ground must be tilled in order to be suitable to give life to plants. These are just a few examples, and it is not a fact by any means, but it helps me to think about the value of tension—it can help one to endure discipline and to anticipate how God is working. Paul clearly tells us, "For the moment all discipline seems painful rather than pleasant, but later it yields the peaceful fruit of righteousness to those who have been trained by it." This is an essential reminder when enduring trials or, better, when being sanctified. The image of bearing fruit is another metaphor that points to John 15—the vine and the branches. John 15:2 (NIV) reads: "He cuts off every branch in me that bears no fruit, while every branch that does bear fruit he prunes." God is the gardener who prunes the branches (his people) who are connected to the vine (Jesus). I also think of the branch bearing fruit in two ways. The metaphor is clear in that branches represent people. As a branch grows, it needs to remain strongly connected to the vine. This main branch grows out further and further as the gardener prunes it. I think it also makes sense to think of the constant offshoots of the branch that God cuts off, leaving stubs along the branch. These stubs represent the offshoots in our lives that just did not pan out. In my own life, for example, I have a degree in business, but I do not have a career in business. Business is a stub on the branch of my life, but it is part of me and certainly part of the way I work and view life. I am not bearing any business fruit, but the fruit I am bearing is informed by business.

Another noteworthy aspect of this pruning metaphor is that an experienced gardener will never damage a fruit tree by pruning it. It may be painful to experience discipline, but it is not damaging. Instead, it is life-giving and maximizes the fruit that one can produce, maximizing one's capacity to glorify God. Fruit-growers make many different cuts in order to help their fruit trees bear fruit successfully. One such cut is the directional cut, which forces the branch to grow in a certain direction. Each cut is purposeful. The metaphor of refining gold has the same connection. A refiner must watch the gold while it is held over the flame. If the gold remains in the fire for just a second too long, the gold will be damaged. The refiner knows the gold is ready when he or she is able to see his or her reflection in it. This is a powerful thought with God as the refiner.

The dynamic of discipline described by Paul is seen in the Old Testament as well. In Isaiah 38, King Hezekiah is struck with an unexplained illness, and Isaiah tells him he will die soon. However, he prays to God to extend his life, and his prayer is answered. After enduring the sickness, Isaiah recounts that Hezekiah said, "Indeed it was for my own peace that I had great bitterness" (Isa 38:17,

NKJV). The king finds the peaceful fruit of righteousness after experiencing discipline. In this case the discipline was sickness, but it can come in many varieties, for different durations, and for different reasons. The overall reason is always holiness, but the micro-reason could be to eliminate a particularly destructive pattern from one's life or to teach one to be patient. Whatever the case may be, the goal is holiness so that God will be glorified.

Proverbs 1:23–33 (NRSV)

> Give heed to my reproof;
> I will pour out my thoughts to you;
>> I will make my words known to
>>> you.
> Because I have called and you refused,
>> have stretched out my hand and
>>> no one heeded,
> and because you have ignored all my
> counsel
>> and would have none of my
>>> reproof,

I also will laugh at your calamity....
    Then they will call upon me, but I
    will not answer;
    they will seek me diligently, but
        will not find me.
Because they hated knowledge
    and did not choose the fear of the
        LORD,
would have none of my counsel,
    and despised all my reproof,
therefore they shall eat the fruit of
their way
    and be sated with their own
        devices.
For waywardness kills the simple,
    and the complacency of fools
        destroys them;
but those who listen to me will be
secure
    and will live at ease, without dread
        of disaster. (Prov 1:23–26,
        28–33)

I think there are two main ways to understand "the fear of the Lord." The first way is to focus on what God *would* do if he is *not* obeyed. This can be helpful, yet its outlook is based on God's wrath. The second way, however, is to focus on what God *will* do if he *is* obeyed. I would suggest that this way is even more helpful because it is a product of a positive, promise-based disposition. The difference is essentially living either afraid of God or expectant of God.

I wanted to include this passage from the book of Proverbs because it shows two paths. If one does not choose to trust God through discipline, that person is a fool. If one does trust God through discipline, that person will gain wisdom and will be secure. It also gives a bit of an introduction to the book of Proverbs. The majority of Proverbs is written by Solomon, who succeeded David, his father, as king of Israel. Proverbs is a book of wisdom, and it contains this well-known verse: "The fear of the LORD is the beginning of knowledge; fools despise wisdom and instruction" (1:7, NRSV).

Solomon must have learned this from his father, as it is also written in Psalm 111. Trusting God and accepting his discipline are the roots of wisdom. Fear of the Lord is a central biblical topic.[13] In fact, Solomon writes about the fear of the Lord in another part of the Bible—the book of Ecclesiastes. Ecclesiastes is famous for its third chapter, which notes that there is an appointed time for everything. However, it is the last chapter that I want to bring to your attention. Ecclesiastes 12:13 (NKJV) reads, "Let us hear the conclusion of the whole matter: Fear God and keep His commandments, for this is man's all." This is how Solomon, "the wisest man who ever lived," sums up how to live in relationship to God. This is a man who had the resources to live any lifestyle imaginable, and this is what he recommends. What does it mean to fear God? Here is my definition: to fear God means to trust that all of his ways are the best ways. Fearing God is, therefore, directly evidenced by keeping his commandments. Trusting that

God's ways are the best ways and obeying those ways allow for a right relationship with God.

One more important point from this passage is that God's people have a choice. As it says in verse 29, some choose to not fear the Lord. In many ways it is the decision to engage in the sanctification process. If one does not trust that God's ways are the best ways and does not obey his ways, one will not be in a right relationship with God. One who does not fear the Lord does not remain or abide in the vine, and apart from the vine one can do nothing: "If you do not remain in me, you are like a branch that is thrown away and withers; such branches are picked up, thrown into the fire and burned" (John 15:6, NIV).

Deuteronomy 8:5–10

> Know then in your heart that, as a man disciplines his son, the LORD your God disciplines you. So you shall keep the commandments of the LORD your God by walking in his ways and by

fearing him. For the LORD your God is bringing you into a good land…. And you shall eat and be full, and you shall bless the LORD your God for the good land he has given you. (Deut 5–7a, 10)

This passage from Deuteronomy is a good way of continuing this exploration of discipline because it looks at the whole picture. It contains similar language to Hebrews 12:5–8 as it mentions discipline and sonship, and to Proverbs 1:29 as it mentions the fear of the Lord. However, I want to emphasize the very first word of the passage: *know*. This is an imperative, and it points back to the renewal of the mind. Horace Stoessel calls this "internalizing the truth."[14] Knowing wholeheartedly that God uses discipline as a tool for sanctification is essential to enduring discipline. Without this knowledge it is natural to think of discipline as punishment without the refining impact. Part of the reason Paul wrote about discipline in his letter to the Hebrews is that he wanted to make sure the Hebrews were not interpreting their sufferings or Paul's own sufferings as something negative. Paul's message carries on to Christians today.

In Deuteronomy 8 the specific truth God is calling his people to know as an indisputable fact is that discipline ensures that one is a child of God. Paul puts this succinctly to the Hebrews: "If you are left without discipline, in which all have participated, then you are illegitimate children and not sons" (Heb 12:8). Discipline is the mark of a child of God—that is perhaps the main reason James connects joy and trials. God's people can be joyful in trials because such trials are confirmation that they are children of God.[15]

Psalm 119:25–32

My soul clings to the dust;
give me life according to your
word!

When I told of my ways, you
answered me;
    teach me your statutes!
Make me understand the way of your
precepts,
        and I will meditate on your
            wondrous works.
My soul melts away for sorrow;
    strengthen me according to your
        word!
Put false ways far from me
    and graciously teach me your law!
I have chosen the way of faithfulness;
    I set your rules before me.
I cling to your testimonies, O LORD;
    let me not be put to shame!
I will run in the way of your
commandments
    when you enlarge my heart!
        (Ps 119:25–32)

The author, most likely David, is describing
a time of distress and a search for the right way to

go—something to trust in. This is part of being human. Especially in this generation, humans have so many options of what and whom to trust and what they should value as important. Some will turn to working excessive hours, completely driven by their own sense of success as they live in the gaze of others and chase after status and reputation. Others will perfect their appearance and buy the best products for skin and hair and go to the gym whenever they have any free time. Many others will turn to alcohol or drugs in an effort to forget instead of pressing on. God gave us his commandments to live by in the midst of so many options, and he gave us the Holy Spirit to guide us. His commandments are not a burden; they are a refuge. This is the same line of thinking presented in Ecclesiastes 12:13. In times of distress and suffering, it is particularly crucial to cling to God as one's rock and refuge—to know and trust that his ways are the best, life-giving, sanctifying ways—and to commit to living in those ways, obeying his commandments. In the psalm above, David begins with a scene of despair, clinging to the dust, but by the end he writes, "I cling to your testimonies, O LORD." God has designed life this way. He has given humans something to turn to in all circumstances, particularly during difficult and confusing times when nothing is making sense. Deuteronomy presents this theme clearly.[16] Walking in his ways is the means of keeping his commandments.

Åke Sander writes about religions as scripts: "Religions, then, are culturally adapted scripts, derived from typical religious experience, that provide ways of life, ways of living in our bodies. They are scripts for how we as human beings should respond to the raw facts of being and living in the world, to the human condition, which is indelibly marked by suffering and death."[17]

Each religion is a script for how to respond to life—life that is marked by suffering. The experience of suffering often forces the sufferer to consider how suffering can be eliminated. Approaches to suffering are found in each major religion. Buddhism, Islam, Hinduism, Judaism, and Christianity have their similarities and differences, but what sets the Judeo-Christian script apart is the emphasis on holiness. Christianity is set apart further by emphasizing right relationship with Jesus Christ as the means for that holiness. At any rate, suffering has been prompting people to look at these scripts for ages. In fact, Buddhism is itself a response to suffering. The Buddha, Siddhartha Gautama, created the tenets of Buddhism based on the way he endured suffering in his own life. My point is that God employs suffering to get his people's attention. C. S. Lewis famously wrote: "God whispers to us in our pleasures, speaks in our conscience, but shouts in our pain."[18] One can then "listen" to God by reading the Bible and trusting in his promises so that they might be refined through their suffering. The remaining sections of this book continue to explore the Christian script, ultimately concluding that trust is the overall theme of the play, if you will. First, however, let us have a look at obedience.

Careful Unreasonableness

So often we mar God's designed influence through us by our self-conscious effort to be consistent and useful. Jesus says that there is only one way to develop spiritually, and that is by concentration on God.... The people who influence us most are not those who buttonhole us and talk to us, but those who live their lives like the stars in heaven and the lilies in the field, perfectly simply and unaffected. Those are the lives that mold us. If you want to be of use to God, get rightly related to Jesus Christ and He will make you of use unconsciously every minute you live.[19]

Having identified God's will for his people (holiness) and his means for achieving it (discipline), the next few sections will focus on practical ways of trusting God, enduring discipline, and staying focused on the sanctification process. Oswald Chambers, a Scottish evangelist from the early twentieth century, gives us a great way of approaching this section on obedience. There are many different perspectives on how we can best please God. Many circles promote evangelism. This is certainly a biblically critical practice for Christians, yet oftentimes this can bring a great deal of pressure on people who may not have an aptitude for it. If one focuses on evangelism and trying to get to a certain number of converts, the original focus on God may begin to fade. In other circles there may be an emphasis on prayer. In a Catholic setting, for instance, there are many ways to pray and worship—Mass, rosary, adoration, breviary, vespers, pilgrimages, etc. Oftentimes these devotional practices can become a sort of competition as well. Just like with evangelism, it can become a way of showing dedication—that one has a certain amount of faith. Chambers is aware of this and wonderfully articulates a helpful perspective: concentrating on God and being rightly related to Jesus Christ are the most important ways of being of use to God. Therefore, one can be of use to God through trusting him, via fearing him and obeying his ways. Ultimately, his way is *the* way, Jesus.

One must abide in the vine in order to bear fruit. One's focus needs to be on Jesus and following him through discipline by trusting, obeying, and waiting for God. That is the path one must walk if one wants to be of use to God. Paul puts it this way when he writes to Timothy: "Now in a great house there are not only vessels of gold and silver but also of wood and clay, some for honorable use, some for dishonorable. Therefore, if anyone cleanses himself from what is dishonorable, he will be a vessel for honorable use, set apart as holy, useful to the master of the house, ready for every good work" (2 Tim

2:20–21). The focus is on relationship. If one cleanses oneself from what is dishonorable, one will be a vessel for God to work through—a channel of God's peace, as Francis of Assisi might say. The vine and the branches metaphor is emphatically important and helpful here. A branch must focus on its relationship with the vine and not its production of fruit. Branches that are not abiding in the vine are burned in the fire.

Simple Obedience

When Jesus demanded voluntary poverty of the rich young man, the young man knew that his only choices were obedience or disobedience. When Levi was called from his tax collecting and Peter from his nets, there was no doubt that Jesus was serious about those calls. They were supposed to leave everything and follow him. When Peter was called to step out onto the stormy sea, he had to get up and risk taking the step. Only one thing was demanded in each of these cases. That was their entrusting themselves to the word of Jesus Christ, believing it to be a stronger foundation than all the securities in the world. The forces that wanted to get between the word of Jesus and obedience were just as great back then as they are today. Reason objected; conscience, responsibility, piety, even the law and the principle of Scripture intervened to inhibit this most extreme, this lawless "enthusiasm." Jesus' call broke all of this and mandated obedience. It was God's own word. Simple obedience was required.[20]

Dietrich Bonhoeffer was a German theologian and pastor during the first half of the twentieth century until his imprisonment and hanging in 1945 as a result of his anti-Nazi stance throughout World War II. Bonhoeffer is well known for the notion of "cheap grace," which he develops in *Discipleship*. For now, however, I am going to focus on his thought regarding "simple obedience." He dedicates an entire chapter to this idea, and the excerpt above serves as the chapter's beginning. Bonhoeffer sharply asserts that even during Jesus' time, the draw to trust in other things was just as strong as it is today. When Jesus called Levi and Peter from their jobs, there was no earthly reason behind their decisions. They chose to follow Jesus because, as Bonhoeffer puts it, they "entrust[ed] themselves to the word of Jesus Christ, believing it to be a stronger foundation than all the securities of the world." This is what initiates simple obedience. A steady job as a fisherman or a tax collector provided a certain amount of security, but nothing is as secure as Jesus Christ. He is the "perfecter of our faith" because of his radical obedience to God: "And being found in human form, he humbled himself by becoming obedient to the point of death, even death on a cross" (Phil

2:8). Obedience can be extremely difficult, but it is a critical aspect of God's will.[21]

One of the major realizations I have had in regard to obedience is that, as Bonhoeffer notes, it is a choice to put one's faith in a certain concept and to act—it is to trust. One can decide to put one's trust in anything: a politician, a product, a diet plan, a religion, a career, or even oneself. Trustworthiness can be based on many different factors, but it is usually based on results. One will start a certain diet because it has been effective for others. One will campaign for a certain candidate because that candidate has carried through on promises while holding another office. My point is that there are reasons why humans logically consider a person or product or plan to be trustworthy. With a careful examination of God's promises and his fulfillment of those promises, one will begin to see why God is trustworthy. Kierkegaard calls it "madness" to follow Jesus, and in the world's view that will always be the case. However, from the perspective of a disciple, it is far from madness—it is the only way. That way is Jesus: the Way, the Truth, and the Life. The next section is dedicated to a discussion of God's promises.

You Don't Have to Know God's Will

Over the decades I've followed him,
Jesus has made something very clear
to me in the Scriptures, the lives of
eminent saints, and my own stumbling
experience: Living in the will of God is
more about knowing and trusting his
specific promises than receiving specific
direction (Hebrews 11:8). It's more
about resting in his sovereignty than
wrestling with my ambiguity (Psalm
131:1–2).[22]

Jon Bloom is a pastor and a frequent
contributor to and co-founder of the popular
ministry Desiring God. Here, he promotes
some of the ideas I have been suggesting, and he

phrases it so well. Bloom so correctly conveys that God has given his people *specific* promises in which they can place their trust. God grants all of his promises.[23]

God presents two promises that I find particularly helpful. The first promise is the Holy Spirit. John 14:15–17 is a prominent passage in Scripture describing this promise. Jesus tells his disciples not to worry when he leaves them because God will send them the Holy Spirit to be their comforter and advocate. This promise extends to all Christians today, and it is part of God's amazing design for Christian life. A quotation from the late Heribert Mühlen, one of my favorite theologians, explains what I mean: "Paul therefore reminds the Galatians that when they began to be Christians, they were granted a life-transforming *experience of the Spirit* which they can continually *recall* and which *permanently* determines their life."[24] This is what Paul writes in Galatians 4:6–7: "And because you are sons, God has sent the Spirit of his Son into our hearts, crying, 'Abba! Father!'

So you are no longer a slave, but a son, and if a son, then an heir through God." Paul writes something similar in many of his letters.[25] The Spirit is a promise that a justified Christian can remember and trust in as a promise fulfilled. This tangible, experiential promise is the foundation of every Christian life and is the seal of God's declaration that one is holy. I look at this promise closely in a recent article.[26] It is essential to understand the Holy Spirit as an active, tangible force within one's life. Moreover, the Holy Spirit gives God's people a different orientation toward suffering, which gives suffering a refining quality. *With* the Holy Spirit, suffering is discipline; *without* the Holy Spirit, suffering is suffering. Scripture scholar Steven Harmon writes that "through the Holy Spirit [believers] have access to the qualitatively different relation to suffering that God has.... God suffers impassibly—entering into suffering without being overcome by it—and so may we."[27] Not only can believers endure suffering, but they can also be refined by it. This different relationship to suffering is present because of the promise of the Holy Spirit.

The second promise I find helpful is that of eternal life. While the promise of the Holy Spirit is something to recall and acts as a foundation, the promise of eternal life is something to look forward to and acts as a future reality. The term I like to use when thinking about the empowering characteristic of this promise is eschatological ontology. Eschatology is the study of the end times, and ontology is the study of being. Therefore, if one has an *eschatological ontology*, one has a state of being rooted in one's belief in what will happen at the end time. In a Christian context this means one's very being and mindset are entrenched in one's belief in eternal life, even to the extent that one realizes that they are living eternally right now. John Zizioulas, an Eastern Orthodox metropolitan, uses the phrase "remembering the future."[28] I find this to be a central Christian state of mind and being. Christians can remember and be assured of a brilliantly bright future ahead.

Paul illustrates this clearly: "For to me to live is Christ, and to die is gain. If I am to live in the flesh, that means fruitful labor for me. Yet which I shall choose I cannot tell. I am hard pressed between the two. My desire is to depart and be with Christ, for that is far better" (Phil 1:21–23). This may seem a little odd at first, but Paul's perspective is a genuine one, deeply rooted in abiding with Christ to the point that he wants to be with Christ directly in heaven. He is not suicidal; he is simply so convinced he will be with Christ when he dies that he is excited for it. He continues: "But to remain in the flesh is more necessary on your account. Convinced of this, I know that I will remain and continue with you all, for your progress and joy in the faith, so that in me you may have ample cause to glory in Christ Jesus, because of my coming to you again" (Phil 1:24–26). What a perspective!

Christians can place their trust in these two promises and so many others because God is trustworthy. Just read Hebrews 11. Paul gives a litany of examples of how God works through people who trust in him. In Hebrews 11 the Greek word *pistei*, a form of *pistis*, is repeated eighteen times and is seemingly always translated as "by faith." To do something by faith means to trust. If you read this passage, think of *trust* when you read *faith*, and consider the great things that happened because of trusting in God. You will read of Abraham's obedience, Sarah's patience, and Moses's trust, but there is so much more. Paul also mentions Gideon, Barak, Samson, Jephthah, David, Samuel, and the prophets, "who through faith subdued kingdoms, worked righteousness, obtained promises, stopped the mouths of lions, quenched the violence of fire, escaped the edge of the sword, out of weakness were made strong, [and] became valiant in battle" (Heb 11:33–34, NKJV). Paul affirms that God's people inherit his promises when they trust in him. Earlier in the same letter, Paul writes: "We do not want you to become lazy, but to imitate those who through faith and patience inherit what has been promised" (Heb 6:12, NIV).

If one identifies one's goal as sanctification and endures discipline through trust by obeying God's commandments and clinging to God's promises, then I truly believe one will be doing God's will. However, one more thing to consider is that it may take a very long time. In the next section I will address the topic of patience. Before making that transition, I highly recommend that you flip toward the end of your Bible and read 2 Peter 1:3–11.

Augustine on Time

Time is not inert. It does not roll through our senses without affecting us. Its passing has remarkable effects on the mind.[29]

These words from Augustine have stuck with me ever since I first read his *Confessions* during my first year of college. I have only recently begun to understand what he meant. Patience is a necessity for developing commitment to trusting and obeying God throughout the sanctification process. Time is needed for the renewal of the mind through the internalization of truth. Letting God achieve his will through us will always take time. However, Christians must realize that God's perfect timing is a blessing, not a burden. It may seem confusing at first, but this design allows one to be actively passive. What I mean by this is that one must embrace Chambers' assertion that "he will make you of use unconsciously every minute you live" if you get rightly related to Jesus Christ. God is the one who acts. Of course, humans can act, but Christians must strive to be focused on being a temple where God can send his Spirit to dwell. They must focus on abiding in the vine by trusting in Jesus wholeheartedly. Only then will they be truly fruitful. To further explain the importance of patience, I have included a series of passages from the book of Isaiah. The Bible is clear and consistent about the role of patience.[30]

Isaiah 64:4

> From of old no one has heard
>> or perceived by the ear,
> no eye has seen a God besides you,
>> who acts for those who wait for
>> him. (Isa 64:4)

This is an incredible truth to behold. *God* will act for those who wait for him. Waiting can be difficult, but I will wait as long as I can if it means God will act through me.

Isaiah 40:28–31

Have you not known? Have you not
heard?
The LORD is the everlasting God,
the Creator of the ends of the
earth.
He does not faint or grow weary;
his understanding is unsearchable.
He gives power to the faint,
and to him who has no might he
increases strength.
Even youths shall faint and be weary,
and young men shall fall
exhausted;
but they who wait for the LORD shall
renew their strength;
they shall mount up with wings
like eagles;

they shall run and not be weary;
  they shall walk and not faint.
    (Isa 40:28–31)

This is another great passage that communicates a crucial characteristic of God—he is everlasting. God is not in a hurry. He will use all the time it takes to sanctify people. As Peter writes: "But do not overlook this one fact, beloved, that with the Lord one day is as a thousand years, and a thousand years as one day" (2 Pet 3:8). If one would embrace eternal life in the present, one might realize why God so emphasizes waiting. God uses time to achieve his will in an eternal context.

Isaiah 49:1–2
  Listen to me, O coastlands,
    and give attention, you peoples
      from afar.
  The LORD called me from the womb,
    from the body of my mother he
      named my name.

He made my mouth like a sharp
sword;
> in the shadow of his hand he hid
> me;
he made me a polished arrow;
> in his quiver he hid me away.
> (Isa 49:1–2)

This verse is similar to Jeremiah 1:5 and should not be brought too far out of context.[31] However, I very much appreciate this verse for its metaphoric value. Metaphors are important to Christianity. Christians are called to be salt, light, and clay, and they are to think about their relationship with God as a sheep to a shepherd and to Jesus as a branch to a vine. This arrow metaphor makes a great deal of sense to me, and I find that it fits in very well with my perspective on God's will. Here is how I would describe the metaphor: a master archer crafts an arrow and puts a mark on it to indicate it is his (justification and seal of the Spirit). He then polishes the arrow (renewal of the mind) and places it in his quiver. Then comes the time when the archer needs to use the arrow. He takes it from his quiver and puts it on his bow. Then he pulls back, putting great tension on the arrow, and takes his perfect aim (sanctification—enduring discipline through trusting in God's plan). Then he takes his shot (God achieves his will through our lives). The metaphor is not flawless by any means, but I find it to be a helpful lens into Christian life and God's will. The tension of the bow on the arrow is necessary for the arrow to have any potential and for the archer to shoot at the target. Similarly, discipline is necessary for God to make his people holy.

One more metaphor that I think deserves mentioning is one I have already mentioned: the refiner's fire. This metaphor is largely from Malachi 3:2–4: "But who can endure the day of his coming, and who can stand when he appears? For he is like a refiner's fire and like fullers' soap. He will sit as a refiner and purifier of silver, and he will purify the sons of Levi and refine them like gold and silver, and they will bring offerings in righteousness to the LORD. Then the offering of Judah and Jerusalem will be pleasing to the LORD as in the days of old and as in former years."

God is a master goldsmith and silversmith, and we are the gold and silver. It is summarized beautifully by verse 4 of "How Firm a Foundation": "When through fiery trials thy pathway shall lie, his grace all-sufficient shall be thy supply; the flame shall not hurt thee, his only design, thy dross to consume and thy gold to refine."[32] This is a great description of the sanctification process, yet there is even more to the metaphor. The responsibilities of a goldsmith add another layer to the profundity of this metaphor. A goldsmith has to place the gold in the hottest part of the fire, watch it the entire time, and the gold is fully refined once the goldsmith can see his or her reflection in the gold. I wanted to share this metaphor again because it has been particularly helpful for me. The penultimate section is dedicated to exploring trust and takes a look at another metaphor.

TRUST AS
GOD'S WILL

Psalm 37:5

Commit your way to the LORD;
    trust in him, and he will act.
    (Ps 37:5)

If I had to pick a motto, this would most likely be it. As a Christian, the one thing I want to do with my life is God's will. When people ask me what I want to do with my life, I often joke that I want to do God's will full-time—but it is true. This verse has helped me immensely to renew my mind and understand the way God has designed his relationship with humanity. This verse can even act as a summary statement for the content of this book, and there are many more.[33]

In his commentary on Psalms 1 to 50, the late Peter Craigie writes the following regarding this verse: "The essence of living faith is concisely described. The acts of commitment and trust function like a trigger, releasing God's capacity to act."[34] This is where God's will and trust become clearly connected. God is the only one that can do God's will; however, he can and will execute his will through his people if they trust in him. So if God is the one doing God's will, what exactly does trusting God consist of? What are practical ways in which trust can be practiced? What are the fruits of trust? My thought is that the practical ways in which trust can be lived out are through obedience and patience, which are sustained by God's promises in the midst of discipline and at all times. And the fruit of trust is uncovering holiness, God's will for all his people. So commit your way to the Lord; trust in him, and he will act!

Jesus is the ultimate example of sanctification because he is holy—not only in his standing with God but also in his disposition. He is the ultimate example of being set apart and trusting and obeying God through suffering. His bond of trust with God was never broken, even throughout his inexpressibly painful passion and crucifixion. Jesus had absolutely the best attitude in the face of suffering and throughout his life on earth. Kevin Vanhoozer observes that "sanctification is ultimately a matter of being translated into the image of the Son, of coming to have the mind—attitude, dispositions and desires—of Christ."[35] The characteristics from the above discussion—patience, obedience, etc.—are exemplified perfectly by Jesus. One can marvel at "the fidelity and trust that [Jesus] himself exhibited in a fully adequate way and that his followers are called upon to share."[36] Studying the life of Jesus is, in many ways, a study of trust.

Amy Peeler gives a strong account of the role of trust as the defining characteristic of Jesus' life. She argues that Jesus' attitude is one of trust, which propels him through trials. She notes that "Jesus displays an attitude of confident trust in God, thus providing a model for the audience of the way in which they should respond to God in the midst of their own difficulties."[37] Trust is the attitude Jesus displays throughout his life. Peeler utilizes much of the letter to the Hebrews and Isaiah 8:17 to discuss Jesus' trust, especially in the midst of suffering. She cites his sinless life as a display of obedient trust, his praying to God as trust, and, critically, his death as his greatest display of trust. Peeler writes that these aspects of Jesus' life "suggest that Jesus' proclamation of trust in God displays the attitude he maintained throughout life, but most emphatically in his death."[38] The trust Jesus shows in his passion by being "obedient to the point of death, even the death of the cross" (Phil 2:8, NKJV) is the summit of his trust. God's goal for the sanctification process is to make his people holy or, in other words, to make his people more like Jesus. God uses discipline to make his people turn to him and trust in him, just as Jesus did. God's people are ultimately sanctified by abiding in a trusting relationship with Jesus.

Trust Law

> A trust is a situation in which property is vested in someone (a trustee), who is under legally recognized obligations, at least some of which are of a proprietary kind, to handle it in a certain way, and to the exclusion of any personal interest. These obligations may arise either by conscious creation by the previous owner of the property (the settlor), or because some other legally significant circumstances are present.[39]

Exploring the concept of trust law can be fruitful for Christian life. Let's say you just won the lottery with a payout of $100,000,000. Arguably, the best way to maximize that money is to allow a wealth manager—an expert in investments—to manage it. He or she will most likely invest the money in a diversified portfolio, including stocks, bonds, and real estate, in order to get the best return. In a similar way, if one thinks of one's life as that $100,000,000, and one wants the best return from one's life, God is the best option as a wealth manager. He knows where we can best contribute to his kingdom on earth and how we can best glorify him at every moment. Therefore, I think it makes sense to think about setting up a trust with God.

This is a solid metaphor for discussing the foundation of Christian life. It has its limits, but I think it provides another helpful lens for thinking about relating to God. God invites all of his people to set up a trust with him. He is the trustee, and his people are settlors. The property the settlor vests in the trustee is the settlor's entire life. It is like a trust fund. Money is vested to a trustee, and that trustee manages it to the very best of his or her ability with no personal interest. However, in this spiritual trust I am describing, God is also a beneficiary because in trusting God with one's life, God will sanctify that person, act through that person, and all of the glory will still go to him.

Therefore, I invite you to set up a trust with God. As with a regular trust, you will not know exactly how the trustee will be managing your property, but you can be assured that it is all working out for your good and that the trustee will make every effort to reach the absolute maximum returns for your life. In this case, the returns are a holy disposition and fruitfulness for the settlor and glory for the trustee. If you want to do God's will, if you want to be sanctified, make a trust with God, and be confident in his management of your life.

CONCLUSION

To summarize this little book, I will leave you with my final plea about trust and some cautions going forward. I want to return to the theme of the renewal of the mind. I would hope that you have gained some insight from these pages, but I would not expect much renewal. That will take time (think of Augustine) and prayer and engagement with most of the themes I have presented. The main point I want to reiterate is that trust is at the center of Christian life. Trust is a gift from God that allows us to activate our belief in him. Trust prevents our own foolishness and enables God's sanctifying work.

In promoting trust to this degree, I fear that it may become too much of a focus and that it will drown out a focus on active participation. Trust is not an excuse. If opportunities come about for glorifying God and proclaiming the name of Jesus, I reckon one should take those opportunities with great enthusiasm. These are opportunities to trust, to put faith in action, not to say, "I'm trying to be patient." Bonhoeffer advocates for Christian life defined by "this-worldliness": "By this-worldliness I mean living unreservedly in life's duties, problems, successes and failures, experiences and perplexities. In so doing we throw ourselves completely into the arms of God, taking seriously, not our own sufferings, but those of God in the world—watching with Christ in Gethsemane."[40] Trust is applicable in all circumstances, whether a long-term confusion or a day-to-day problem, whether at home or in a different country. Trust is a gift that is not bound by any situation or context, yet it binds one to Christ.

Moreover, trust is not something to be idolized. A Christian must fix his or her eyes on Christ. Trust is an exceedingly useful way of doing that. Trust is a means of worshiping

God and of going beyond oneself, establishing one's life in God's Word and God's promises. Trust is a way of affirming Isaiah 55:9: "For as the heavens are higher than the earth, so are [God's] ways higher than your ways and [God's] thoughts than your thoughts." Trust is the best response to all of God's sanctifying initiatives.

I also want to once again consider the role of trust in Jesus' life. Scripture shows us that Jesus' own life was characterized by trust. Many passages show Jesus' reliance on the Father, his unfailing devotion to the Father's will, and his confidence in the Father's word. Again, Peeler writes: "All of these factors strongly suggest that Jesus' proclamation of trust in God displays the attitude he maintained throughout life, but most emphatically in his death."[41] She emphasizes Isaiah 8:17, which corresponds to Hebrews 2:10–13. Those verses are worth a look, but for now let us consider John 12:27 (NIV): "Now my soul is troubled, and what shall I say? 'Father, save me from this hour?' But for this purpose I came to this hour. Father, glorify your name." Jesus' reaction to suffering is so humanly authentic at first. He does not want to experience the suffering he is destined to face. However, Jesus' attention shifts to what his suffering will achieve. As Heinrich Meyer puts it: "But immediately this wish, resulting from natural dread of suffering and death, yields to the victorious consciousness of His great destiny."[42] I truly believe Christians today must follow this example in the face of their own suffering. To trust is to have this "victorious consciousness," knowing that God disciplines his people for their sanctification and his glory, knowing that God's ways are perfect, his timing is perfect, and remembering the future!

My use of the word *trust* throughout this book has been as a comprehensive term. I like to think of trust in this way because I think it is the bridge between faith and practice, action, and life. Trust is faith in action. Patience, obedience, and knowing God's promises are all ways of putting faith in action, and there are many more ways, such as love, hope, forgiveness, compassion, praise, gratitude, worship, prayer, and active church membership. All of these ignite faith in God and keep one abiding in Jesus Christ. Trust is my own way of summarizing all these aspects of Christian life. The defining characteristic of a disciple of Christ has been described in two ways by two of my dialogue partners above. J. C. Ryle writes that "sanctification, again, is the only sure mark of election."[43] Dietrich Bonhoeffer writes that "suffering becomes the identifying mark of a follower of Christ."[44] These are both essential attributes of following Christ. From my perspective, however, the defining characteristic of a disciple of Christ is trust in Christ.

In closing, I offer to you a prayer by Pierre Teilhard de Chardin, a French Jesuit priest, philosopher, and geologist of the first half of the twentieth century. This prayer is perhaps the cornerstone regarding my thoughts about trust and God's will. It came to me at a crucial time when I was actively searching for God's will, becoming increasingly discouraged that

I could not find it. However, this prayer, this perspective, helped me to realize that God is truly in control and that my role is to surrender to that control—to vest my entire life in that control and live in God's eternal timeframe, trusting Jesus Christ at all times.

Patient Trust

Above all, trust in the slow work of
God.
We are quite naturally impatient in
everything
    to reach the end without delay.
We should like to skip the
intermediate stages.
We are impatient of being on the way
to something unknown, something
new.
And yet it is the law of all progress
    that it is made by passing through
    some stages of instability—
    and that it may take a very long
        time.

And so I think it is with you;
    your ideas mature gradually—let
        them grow,
    let them shape themselves,
        without undue haste.
Don't try to force them on,
    as though you could be today
        what time
    (that is to say, grace and
        circumstances
    acting on your own good will)
    will make of you tomorrow.
Only God could say what this new
spirit
    gradually forming within you will
        be.
Give Our Lord the benefit of believing
    that his hand is leading you,
    and accept the anxiety of feeling
        yourself
    in suspense and incomplete.[45]

NOTES

[1] Søren Kierkegaard, *Training in Christianity*, trans. Walter Lowrie (New York: Vintage Books, 2004), 49.

[2] Gordon T. Smith, "Conversion and Redemption," in *The Oxford Handbook of Evangelical Theology*, ed. Gerald R. McDermott (Oxford: Oxford University Press, 2010), 214.

[3] I am thankful to John Piper for his explanations of these topics. See Heb 10:14.

[4] If you are unsure of this, I encourage you to look into it. See N. T. Wright, *Justification: God's Plan and Paul's Vision* (Downer's Grove: InterVarsity Press, 2009).

[5] Dietrich Bonhoeffer, *Discipleship*, vol. 4 of *Dietrich Bonhoeffer Works*, ed. Geffrey B. Kelly and John D. Godsey, trans. Reinhard Krauss and Barbara Green (Minneapolis: Fortress Press, 2003), 77.

[6] Kierkegaard, *Training in Christianity*, 49.

[7] See Mal 3:2–4; Matt 5:48; John 17:17–19; Rom 6:22; Phil 3:8–12; 1 Thess 3:11–13; 5:23; 2 Thess 2:13; 1 Cor 3:17; 2 Tim 2:20–21; 1 Pet 1:13–21.

[8] See Jon 1–3.

[9] George Gaffga, *Fields of Grace: Devotional Thoughts* (Sarasota: First Edition Design, 2013), 151.

[10] J. C. Ryle, *Holiness (Abridged): Its Nature, Hindrances, Difficulties, and Roots* (Chicago: Moody Publishers, 2010), 81.

[11] I am grateful to Andrew Case for this line of thinking.

[12] Ryle, *Holiness*, 107. Also see Rom 3.

[13] See Deut 6:2; 10:12–22; Josh 4:23–24; 1 Sam 15:24; Ps 112; Prov 14; 15:33; Acts 9:31; Col 3:22. Proverbs and Deuteronomy are particularly saturated with this topic.

[14] Horace E. Stoessel, "Notes on Romans 12:1–2: The Renewal of the Mind and Internalizing the Truth," *Interpretation: A Journal of Bible and Theology* 17/2 (1963): 161.

[15] See the following verses for more links between suffering and discipline: Job 5:17; Pss 50:16–17; 94:12–13; 119:50; Prov 3:11–12; 5:23; 6:23; 12:1; 23:12–13; 13:1; Acts 5:41; Rom 5:1–5; Rom 8:17; 1 Pet 4:12–13; Rev 3:19.

[16] See Deut 6:2; 8:6, 11; 20:16.

[17] Åke Sander, "The Phenomenological Method Revisited: Towards Comparative Studies and

Non-theological Interpretations of the Religious Experience," *Argument: Biannual Philosophical Journal* 4/1 (2014): 19.

[18] C. S. Lewis, *The Problem of Pain* (San Francisco: HarperCollins, 2001), 91.

[19] Oswald Chambers, *My Utmost for His Highest* (Uhlrichsville, OH: Barbour, 1963), May 18.

[20] Bonhoeffer, *Discipleship*, 77.

[21] See Gen 26:4–5; Exod 19:5; 1 Sam 15; Deut 11–13; 28; Jer 7:23; Ezek 36:25–30; Zech 6:15; John 3:36; Acts 5:12–32; Heb 5:7–10.

[22] Jon Bloom, "You Don't Have to Know God's Will," *Desiring God*, 30 May 2016[not exactly sure what this is…from a website? If so, need link].

[23] See Exod 6:1; Josh 21:45; John 14:15–17; Rom 15:8–13; 2 Cor 1:19–22; 7:1; Gal 3:15–29; Heb. 6:11–20.

[24] Heribert Mühlen, *A Charismatic Theology: Initiation in the Spirit* (London: Burns and Oates, 1978), 48.

[25] See Rom 5:1–5; 8; 2 Cor 1:21–22; 5:5; Eph 1:11–14; Titus 3:4–7. Also see Acts 2, especially vv. 29–41.

[26] Timothy Nagy, "Conversion vs. Initiation: Recovering the Initial Christian Experience in a Catholic Context," *Pneuma* 40/1–2 (2018): 192–211.

[27] Steven R. Harmon, "Hebrews 2:10–18," *Interpretation* 59/4 (2005): 406.

[28] John D. Zizioulas, *Remembering the Future: An Eschatological Ontology* (London: T & T Clark, 2009).

[29] Augustine of Hippo, *Confessions*, trans. Henry Chadwick (Oxford: Oxford University Press, 2008), 60.

[30] See Pss 25; 27:14; 37; 62:1–7; 130; Isa 25:9; 30:18; Lam 3:25–26; Mic 7:7; Rom 8:23–25; 9:27–28; Gal 5:5; Heb 6:15; Jas 5:7–11.

[31] Jer. 1:5: "Before I formed you in the womb I knew you, and before you were born I consecrated you; I appointed you a prophet to the nations." As with Isa 29:1–2, this verse describes God's selection of a prophet and should not be directly applied to all lives.

[32] *Hymns of Faith* (London: Scripture Union and C.S.S.M., 1964), 330.

[33] See Pss 1, 20, 22, 31, 37, 40, 56, 115, 118; Prov 3:5-8; 16:20; 28:25; 29:25; Isa 12:2; 26:4; 50:10; Jer 17:7–8; 39:18.

[34] Peter C. Craigie, *Psalms 1–50*, vol. 19 (Waco: Word, 1983), 297.

[35] Kevin J. Vanhoozer, "Translating Holiness: Forms of Word, Writ and Righteousness," *International Journal of Systematic Theology* 13/44 (2011): 398.

[36] Harold W. Attridge and Helmut Koester, *The Epistle to the Hebrews: A Commentary on the Epistle to the Hebrews*, Hermeneia: A Critical and Historical Commentary on the Bible (Philadelphia: Fortress Press, 1989), 356.

[37] Amy L. B. Peeler, *You Are My Son: The Family of God in the Epistle to the Hebrews* (London: Bloomsbury T&T Clark, 2014), 89. This quotation is from footnote 84.

[38] Ibid., 91.

[39] Simon Gardner, *An Introduction to the Law of Trusts*, Clarendon Law Series (Oxford: Oxford University Press, 2003), 2.

[40] Dietrich Bonhoeffer, *Letters and Papers from Prison*, ed. Eberhard Bethge (New York: Macmillan, 1967), 202. Also see Kierkegaard, *Training in Christianity*, 57–61. Kierkegaard's thought of contemporaneousness is exceptionally thought-provoking.

[41] Peeler, *You Are My Son*, 91.

[42] Heinrich August Wilhelm Meyer, William P. Dickson, William Stewart, Frederick Crombie, and Gottlieb Lünemann, *Critical and Exegetical Commentary on the New Testament* (Edinburgh: T&T Clark, 1873), 163.

[43] Ryle, *Holiness*, 51.

[44] Bonhoeffer, *Discipleship*, 89.

[45] Pierre Teilhard de Chardin, "Patient Trust," in *Hearts on Fire: Praying with Jesuits*, ed. Michael Harter, SJ (St. Louis: Institute of Jesuit Sources, 1993), 102–103.

www.ingramcontent.com/pod-product-compliance
Lightning Source LLC
Chambersburg PA
CBHW070623050426
42450CB00011B/3113